DATE DUE

ROOTING FOR
THE HOME TEAM
Sports in the 1800s

DAILY LIFE IN AMERICA IN THE 1800s

ROOTING FOR THE HOME TEAM
Sports in the 1800s

by

Zachary Chastain

Mason Crest Publishers

MASON CREST PUBLISHERS INC.
370 Reed Road
Broomall, Pennsylvania 19008
(866)MCP-BOOK (toll free)
www.masoncrest.com

First Printing
9 8 7 6 5 4 3 2 1

Library of Congress Cataloging-in-Publication Data

Chastain, Zachary.
  Rooting for the home team : sports in the 1800s / by Zachary Chastain.
     p. cm. — (Daily life in america in the 1800s)
  Includes bibliographical references and index.
  ISBN 978-1-4222-1786-3 (hardcover)   ISBN (series) 978-1-4222-1774-0
  ISBN 978-1-4222-1859-4 (pbk.)   ISBN (pbk. series) 978-1-4222-1847-1
  1. Sports—United States—History—19th century. 2. Professional sports—United States—History—19th century. 3. United States—Social conditions—19th century. I. Title.
  GV875.A1C54 2011
  796.0973'09034—dc22
                              2010028158

Produced by Harding House Publishing Service, Inc.
www.hardinghousepages.com
Interior Design by MK Bassett-Harvey.
Cover design by Torque Advertising + Design.
Printed in USA by Bang Printing.

Contents

Introduction

History can too often seem a parade of distant figures whose lives have no connection to our own. It need not be this way, for if we explore the history of the games people play, the food they eat, the ways they transport themselves, how they worship and go to war—activities common to all generations—we close the gap between past and present. Since the 1960s, historians have learned vast amounts about daily life in earlier periods. This superb series brings us the fruits of that research, thereby making meaningful the lives of those who have gone before.

The authors' vivid, fascinating descriptions invite young readers to journey into a past that is simultaneously strange and familiar. The 1800s were different, but, because they experienced the beginnings of the same baffling modernity were are still dealing with today, they are also similar. This was the moment when millennia of agrarian existence gave way to a new urban, industrial era. Many of the things we take for granted, such as speed of transportation and communication, bewildered those who were the first to behold the steam train and the telegraph. Young readers will be interested to learn that growing up then was no less confusing and difficult then than it is now, that people were no more in agreement on matters of religion, marriage, and family then than they are now.

We are still working through the problems of modernity, such as environmental degradation, that people in the nineteenth century experienced for the first time. Because they met the challenges with admirable ingenuity, we can learn much from them. They left behind a treasure trove of alternative living arrangements, cultures, entertainments, technologies, even diets that are even more relevant today. Students cannot help but be intrigued, not just by the technological ingenuity of those times, but by the courage of people who forged new frontiers, experimented with ideas and social arrangements. They will be surprised by the degree to which young people were engaged in the great events of the time, and how women joined men in the great adventures of the day.

When history is viewed, as it is here, from the bottom up, it becomes clear just how much modern America owes to the genius of ordinary people, to the labor of slaves and immigrants, to women as well as men, to both young people and adults. Focused on home and family life, books in this series provide insight into how much of history is made within the intimate spaces of private life rather than in the remote precincts of public power. The 1800s were the era of the self-made man and women, but also of the self-made communities. The past offers us a plethora of heroes and heroines together with examples of extraordinary collective action from the Underground Railway to the creation of the American trade union movement. There is scarcely an immigrant or ethic organization in America today that does not trace its origins to the nineteenth century.

This series is exceptionally well illustrated. Students will be fascinated by the images of both rural and urban life; and they will be able to find people their own age in these marvelous depictions of play as well as work. History is best when it engages our imagination, draws us out of our own time into another era, allowing us to return to the present with new perspectives on ourselves. My first engagement with the history of daily life came in sixth grade when my teacher, Mrs. Polster, had us do special projects on the history of the nearby Erie Canal. For the first time, history became real to me. It has remained my passion and my compass ever since.

The value of this series is that it opens up a dialogue with a past that is by no means dead and gone but lives on in every dimension of our daily lives. When history texts focus exclusively on political events, they invariably produce a sense of distance. This series creates the opposite effect by encouraging students to see themselves in the flow of history. In revealing the degree to which people in the past made their own history, students are encouraged to imagine themselves as being history-makers in their own right. The realization that history is not something apart from ourselves, a parade that passes us by, but rather an ongoing pageant in which we are all participants, is both exhilarating and liberating, one that connects our present not just with the past but also to a future we are responsible for shaping.

—Dr. John Gillis, Rutgers University
Professor of History Emeritus

1800   1801   1803   1804

1800 The Library of Congress is established.

1801 Thomas Jefferson is elected as the third President of the United States.

1804 Journey of Lewis and Clark—Lewis and Clark lead a team of explorers westward to the Columbia River in Oregon.

1803 Louisiana Purchase—The United States purchases land from France and begins westward exploration.

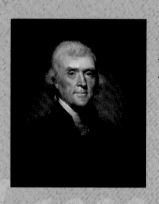

1825   1834   1838   1839

1834 The modern sport of lacrosse is invented, based off of a sport played by North American Indians.

1838 Trail of Tears—General Winfield Scott and 7,000 troops force Cherokees to walk from Georgia to a reservation set up for them in Oklahoma (nearly 1,000 miles). Around 4,000 Native Americans die during the journey.

1839 The first camera is patented by Louis Daguerre.

1825 The Erie Canal is completed—This allows direct transportation between the Great Lakes and the Atlantic Ocean.

1810

1810 The first interracial boxing match takes place, between Tom Cribb (from Great Britain) and Tom Molineaus (from the US).

1812

1812 War of 1812—Fought between the United States and the United Kingdom.

1820

1820 Missouri Compromise—Agreement passes between pro-slavery and abolitionist groups. It states that all the Louisiana Purchase territory north of the southern boundary of Missouri (except for Missouri) will be free states, and the territory south of that line will be slave.

1823

1823 Monroe Doctrine—States that any efforts made by Europe to colonize or interfere with land owned by the United States will be viewed as aggression and require military intervention.

1823 Roller skates are patented by R. J. Tylers.

1840

1840 The first recorded bowling match in the United States is held in New York City.

1844

1844 First public telegraph line in the world is opened—between Baltimore and Washington.

1845

1848 Seneca Falls Convention—Feminist convention held for women's suffrage and equal legal rights.

1848

1845 The New York Knickerbockers are the first organized baseball club.

1848(–58) California Gold Rush—Over 300,000 people flock to California in search of gold.

1861

1861(-65) Civil War —Fought between the Union and Confederate states.

1862

1862 Emancipation Proclamation—Lincoln states that all slaves in Union states are to be freed.

1865

1865 Thirteenth Amendment to the United States Constitution—Officially abolishes slavery across the country.

1865 President Abraham Lincoln is assassinated on April 15.

1867

1867 United States purchases Alaska from Russia.

Time Line

1877

1877 Great Railroad Strike—Often considered the country's first nationwide labor strike.

1878

1878 Thomas Edison patents the phonograph on February 19.

1878 Thomas Edison invents the light bulb on October 22.

1884

1884 First baseball World Series takes place.

1886

1886 The Statue of Liberty is dedicated on October 28.

1869

1869 Trans-
continental
Railroad
completed on
May 10.

1869 First
international
cricket match
is held in San
Francisco.

1869 Football
is invented in
New Jersey.

1870

1870 Fifteenth
Amendment to
the United States
Constitution—Prohibits
any citizen from being
denied to vote based
on their "race, color, or
previous condition of
servitude."

1870 Baseball
is titled "the
national game"
by the New
York Times.

1870 Christmas is
declared a national
holiday.

1876

1876 Alexander
Graham Bell invents
the telephone.

1876 The
"Intercollegiate
Football Association,"
the first rugby
organization in the
United States, is
formed.

1890

1890
Wounded
Knee
Massacre—
Last battle
in the
American
Indian
Wars.

1892

1892 Ellis
Island is
opened to
receive
immigrants
coming into
New York.

1892 The
first
public
basketball
game is
played.

1896

1896 Plessy vs.
Ferguson—
Supreme Court
case that rules
that racial
segregation is
legal as long as
accommodations
are kept equal.

1896 Henry
Ford builds his
first combustion-
powered vehicle,
which he
names the Ford
Quadricycle.

1898

1898 The
Spanish-
American
War—The
United States
gains control
of Cuba, Puerto
Rico, and the
Philippines.

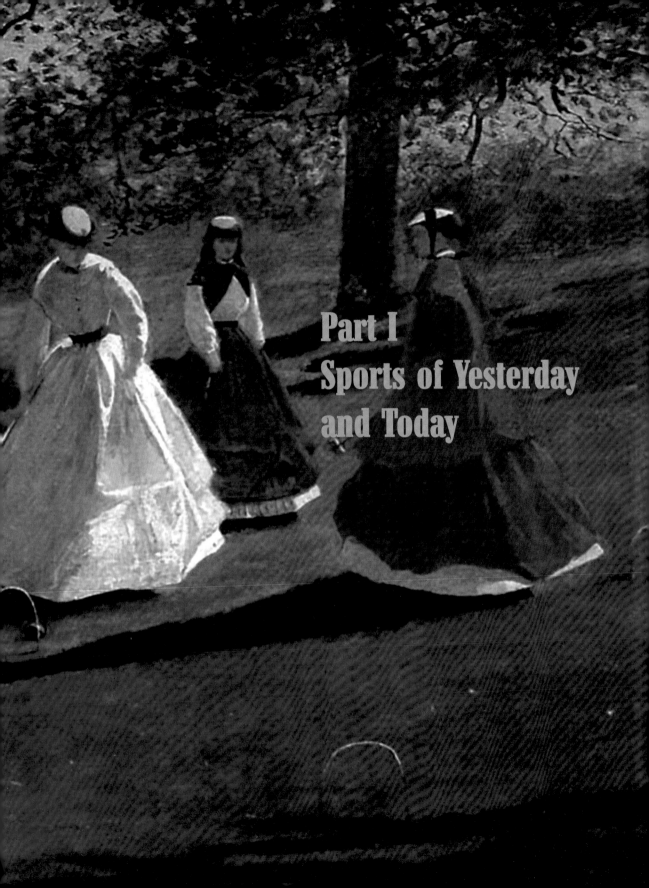

Part I
Sports of Yesterday
and Today

Some people have called sports the "glue" that holds a society together. When politics, race, and economics threaten to split a nation, the one thing people can agree on is often sports. No matter the differences, no matter the rivalries, sports offer a shared experience and a level playing field.

To gain some perspective on sports today, think about these statistics: in 2008, the population of the United States was about 304 million. That same year, 148 million people tuned in to watch the NFL's (National Football League's) championship game, called the "Super Bowl." That's almost half the nation! Also, think about this: the average NBA (National Basketball Association) player earns over $5 million a year, with some player making as much as $20 million in a year. Meanwhile, the average U.S. school teacher, on the other hand, makes $52,000.

Obviously, sports are important to Americans today. And the sports we love and play today are often rooted in our past.

We often assume that the games we play today have existed for hundreds of years, but that's not always true. Many games today were less popular in the 1800s, or just beginning to gain followers. And many of the most well-known games of the 1800s are hardly played at all today!

Most historians believe that tennis originated in France in the 12th century, but the ball was then struck with the palm of the hand. In the early 1870s, a game called "sticky" was developed in England that looked much like modern tennis, and by 1874, the first tennis games were being played in the United States.

Rugby and the "Mob Style" Game

In 1876, the "Intercollegiate Football Association" was officially formed and rugby was born in America. Don't be confused—the word "football" was being used a lot in those days to refer to many different games. In this case, Americans were using the word "football" to refer to the game we know today as "rugby." Leaders from the universities at Yale, Harvard, Princeton, and Columbia decided to keep the rules they liked best, rules that allowed players to carry the ball and have more physical contact. In England, these rules had been made popular at one school in particular, a school called "Rugby," and that's where the sport got its name.

Rugby was a rougher game than soccer, and many Americans objected to the game because they thought it was too violent. But many colleges in the Northeast favored the game, and so rugby kept the rougher, mob-style play that had been popular for so many centuries.

"Mob-style" play refers to the pushing and fighting for the ball that is allowed in rugby, especially in what is called a rugby "scrum." In a scrum, players from each team lock arms with one another and form two rows standing opposite each other. The ball is then dropped between the two lines, and they fight for it. In many ways, this part of the game looks like a battle between two armies.

In the 1800s, the game was significantly more dangerous than it is today. Injuries were common. Over the years, new rules were added to make the game safer and more acceptable to society.

Cricket

Very few Americans today have even heard of cricket, and even fewer know how to play the game. It may surprise you that cricket was, at one time, one of the most popular sports in the United States.

Cricket is a lot like the game we know as baseball, but with major differences. There is a batting team and a fielding team, and the batting team tries to earn points, while the fielding team tries to stop them. Just like baseball, they switch sides after one team gets the other team "out"—or, as they say in cricket, after one team "dismisses" the other. Cricket is a more technical game than baseball. There are more ways to earn points, more ways to "dismiss" someone, and games can go on for much longer than in baseball. Cricket requires a cricket pitch (field), and very particular equipment, including a cricket ball, cricket bat, wicket, stumps, and bails.

Cricket came to the United States with British settlers in the early 1700s. The sport was most popular on the East Coast, where connections to Europe were strongest. Like many sports in the 1800s, cricket was concentrated in cities and at universities. Clubs sprang up in the cities where there were the most spectators and interested players: St. Louis, Boston, New York, Detroit, Baltimore, and especially Philadelphia all had cricket clubs.

Following the Civil War, however, baseball had become so popular that cricket clubs began to convert to the faster-paced game or they shut down entirely. Only a few clubs survived, and those that did usually played overseas against English teams.

Croquet

Croquet has become a sort of joke among many people today. When you imagine the game, you may think of rich ladies and gentlemen dressed in their finest clothes prancing about with mallets. In some ways this is an accurate picture of croquet in the 1800s. But by the end of the 1800s, Americans had added a more fast-paced, competitive edge to the game.

Like so many games, croquet came from England. The basic game is this: players use mallets to hit balls between metal gates, called "wickets," that are stuck into the ground. When the Routledge Handbook of Croquet was published in England in 1861, it didn't take long for the Americans to get hold of the rulebook and the popularity of the sport skyrocketed. Especially popular among the wealthy, it allowed women and men to play a sport together, a rare occurrence in those days. Women especially loved the game.

The English were very particular about the surface on which the game was played. They liked a well cared for lawn of short grass. But the American form of the game evolved so that it could be played on hard-packed dirt. This made it easier to play anywhere. The Americans used more narrow wickets and shorter mallets and added a wooden barricade around the court to keep balls from going out of bounds.

Boxing

Boxing has a long and violent history in the United States. Like many modern sports, boxing has its origins in ancient Greece and Rome. At least, the Greeks and Romans were the first recorded cultures to set rules and guidelines for their boxing matches. Boxing in its most basic form—two fight-

By the end of the 1800s, some boxing matches were attended by members of "high-society," including ladies.

ers using their bare hands in combat—is likely much older than even the Greeks.

In the United States, a form of bare-knuckle boxing called "prize fighting" was most popular in the early 1800s. Adopted from the British, prize fights were fought between two competitors of about the same weight, with a cash prize going to the winner. Early in the century, boxing had very little organization and very little regulation. In fact, many people didn't consider boxing a sport at all. For them, the bloodshed and the occasional deaths in the ring made boxing far too gruesome to be taken seriously as a sport.

But boxing had an enduring appeal to average Americans. Especially in the cities that exploded in size in the late 1800s, people enjoyed watching the best fighter from their neighborhood fight the best fighter from another. Or, as the sport became more organized, a fighter from a Southern state might challenge someone from a Northern state.

Many times, boxing had to be taken "underground" because local laws prohibited it. Boxers and their organizers soon realized that if they wanted to continue their sport they needed to put some rules into place—no hitting below the belt, no hitting an opponent who was "down" in the ring, and a knockdown meant the round was over. These simple rules, along with the development of better boxing gloves, made boxing more acceptable to society at large.

JOE LANNON.

JAKE KILRAIN.

JEM SMITH.

IKE WEIR.

EXTRA! EXTRA!

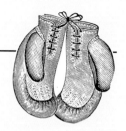

THE SPRINGFIELD WEEKLY REPUBLICAN
SATURDAY, OCTOBER 23, 1858

The Grand Game of Fisticuffs.

There seems to be an element of human nature that delights in brutality for it's own sake. For months we have had notes of preparation, and Heenan, "the Benicia boy," the representative of Yankeedom, and Morrisey, the favorite of the foreign "fancy," have been in process of scientific training, under careful diet and regimen and severe exercise, until they have been freed from superfluous flesh and had their muscles hardened like iron—all this in order that the world might see which would stand up longest under the fists of the other, and thus vindicate his title to what is called "the championship of America." This manifestation of the "muscle movement" that we cannot bring ourselves to "fancy."

The sporting men of the whole country have been intensely interested in this encounter, and it is said that large sums of money were staked on the result. Well, we don't care a penny which beats the other, and the telegraph will doubtless give us the earliest news. Indeed it is said a flight of carrier pigeons has been engaged to convey the earliest intelligence to Buffalo, whence the telegraph wires will diffuse it to an expectant nation.

It is said there is no law by which these brutal exhibitions can be prevented. There should be laws which shall treat prizefighting as dueling is treated, and punish for a challenge or preparation to fight. The mystery to us is that men are found, and by thousands too, who consider this sort of thing "sport," who go long distances at great expense of time and money to see two brutes pummel each other, batter each other's noses, smash each other's eyes, break each other's ribs, and come as near to driving the soul out of the body as is possible and yet escape the guilt of absolute murder.

If human nature is a cross between the bull-dog and hyena we can understand it, but not otherwise. It is quite time that the human race should find it's amusement in something a little less brutal, and test its muscle in a more harmless way.

Horse Racing

Horse racing also has a long history in the United States—so long, in fact, that the first race dates back to 1665. More than three hundred tracks were operating in the United States by 1890, and in 1894, the American Jockey Club was formed. ("Jockey" is the word used for a professional horse rider.)

Horse racing hasn't changed much since the 1800s. Just like today, nineteenth-century horse races were closely connected to gambling. Other sports have been improved by technology in the twentieth and twenty-first centuries, but horse racing relies on breeding more than harnesses, bits, and horseshoes. For centuries, humans have paid close attention to what kinds of horses perform best at different tasks. Some horses are suited to long-distance endurance, some to hard labor, and others can move very fast over relatively short distances. This last quality is what breeders look for in a racing horse.

By the 1800s, the dominant form of horse racing was fast-paced, short-distance racing. The matches were intense and entertaining. Men and women (usually men) placed bets on their favorite horse and then stood by to cheer and scream as their horse and jockey raced around the oval-shaped flat track. Horse racing grew in popularity as many newspapers began to cover races. The press brought a new level of fame to successful horses and their riders. With more attention came more money, meaning the Jockey Club needed to enforce new rules. They introduced professional bookmakers who would keep track of finish times and scores, as well as other standards of order and discipline.

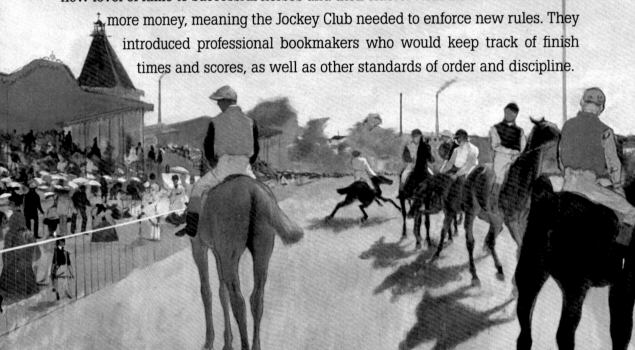

EXTRA! EXTRA!

Newark, New Jersey, 1846

The State of New Jersey has passed an Act to prevent Horse-Racing in our state. The new law reads as follows:

Be it enacted by the Senate and General Assembly of the state of New Jersey, That all wagers and bets which shall be laid, betted or made, on the racing, running, pacing or trotting of horses, mares, or geldings, and all promises, agreements, notes, bills, bonds, contracts, judgments, mortgages or other securities or conveyances, which shall be made, given, granted, drawn, entered into or executed by any person or persons, where the whole or any part of the consideration thereof shall be for any money, goods, chattels or other thing, won, laid or betted on the racing, running, pacing or trotting of horses, mares or geldings, shall be utterly void and of none effect.

INCREDIBLE INDIVIDUAL
Pierre de Coubertin, Founder of the Modern Olympics

Born in 1863 to a noble family in France, de Coubertin grew up in a world of wealth and privilege. He had many opportunities to become a rich man himself, both through government service, the military, or through investments of his father's money. But instead he chose the academic life.

Pierre had an amazing mind. He excelled at school and became very interested in education—especially physical education and how physical activity was important to a person's growth. His interest in sports led him to imagine a new, fantastic possibility: an international competition of athletes. In many ways, the idea was actually quite old. After all, the Greeks had formed the first Olympic games as early as 776 BCE! But Pierre's vision would reach beyond the borders of any one nation. Unlike the ancient Greek games, Pierre wanted to bring together people of many nations and many languages.

He was not alone. The idea for an international competition of athletes also excited the imaginations of two wealthy Greek cousins, Evangelis and Konstantinos Zappas, as well as an English doctor, William Penny Brooke. Each brought a certain expertise to the table, but it was Pierre's passion and his philosophy that drove them onward. In 1894, they held a meeting in Paris to plan the first modern Olympics, which would be held in Athens, Greece.

It worked, but not without much struggle. Wars in Europe had left bitterness between the French and Germans, each threatening to boycott the games. Americans and other nations had to be convinced that the cost of sending athletes overseas was worthwhile. In the end, however, they were convinced. Fourteen nations and 241 athletes participated in the games. There were nine events, including athletics, cycling, fencing, gymnastics, shooting, swimming, tennis, weightlifting, and wrestling. The Olympic Games had been born. As Pierre himself once said: "The important thing in life is not the triumph but the struggle, the essential thing is not to have conquered but to have fought well."

The first modern Olympic Games were held in 1896 in Greece. This photograph shows the audience entering the stadium on the first day.

Lacrosse

In many ways, lacrosse is the only truly "American" sport. When European settlers arrived in the "New World" in the 1600s, they found that some of the native people played a unique game with sticks and a ball. Often the game involved hundreds of tribesmen and lasted from sunrise to sunset—a lot different from the modern form of lacrosse.

But the basics were already in place, and Europeans quickly fell in love with the beautiful sport. They started observing more carefully how the Natives played the game. Different tribes used different sticks to handle the ball. Some attached nets to their sticks, while others hollowed out the wide ends, making their sticks look like enormous spoons. They used large trees, bushes, rocks, or even wooden posts for goals. By the end of the nineteenth century, it was gaining popularity in Montreal, Canada, and a few communities throughout the Northeastern states.

Different tribes used different sticks, but in whatever form, lacrosse was a popular Native sport across much of the eastern half of North America.

Part II
The Rise of the
Major Sports

Although hundreds of sports are played in America today, there are a few that have risen through the ranks to earn highest honors. These are the sports that are most often shown on TV, the ones that are covered in the media, and the ones taught in school gym classes.

Soccer

Soccer has a strange place in the history of the United States. The game that Americans call soccer is called "football" everywhere else in the world, and originally, soccer was called football in the United States too. In the late 1800s in American, however, football split into two additional games—rugby and American football (called "gridiron" at the time.) But it all began with soccer.

Unfortunately for soccer, the popularity of the new rules that created rugby and American football took attention away from the traditional kicking game. It wouldn't be until the 1990s that soccer really regained its importance in the United States. And with America's victory at the 2010 World Cup, American soccer players have finally taken their place among the rest of the world's teams.

Soccer has a long history. Like most early sports, the rules changed from region to region. The number of players on a team, the size and shape of the ball, how to score points: none of these were fixed in place until much later. But the basics were in place. Soccer, then as now, was a game in which a ball was moved by a team from one end of a field to another, using mostly players' feet. No one knows where the game began exactly, or how the rules evolved, but what we do know is that by the 1800s, soccer was being played primarily in Britain—but it was spreading.

Soccer clubs in both the United States and Britain began to appear in the 1800s, usually among the wealthy. Prep schools and elite colleges like Princeton, Harvard, Brown, and Yale were where soccer first became popular in America. Some form of the game had existed since colonists arrived in the 1600s, but rarely did the common person have enough leisure time to play organized sports. The college campus provided the perfect setting for organized sports to thrive: lots of rich young men with time to spend on games.

As college teams increased their skills by playing among themselves on campus, a new desire was born for competition outside the college walls.

Matches between colleges were battles for pride. But there was a problem: who would decide the rules? Each team had its own unique way of playing the game. A common set of rules was needed.

So, in both Britain and the United States, meetings were held between representatives from the various colleges to decide the new rules. The result of these meetings was the creation of a new game, rugby, in which carrying the ball was allowed, along with other physical contact. (In the United States, rugby eventually became American football, the passing,

The Cambridge rules for soccer were first recorded in 1848. No rules were universally adopted until 1863 when the Cambridge rules were revised by a committee.

tackling, and "touchdown" sport we know today.)

Meanwhile, the many fans of traditional football saw their kicking game lose popularity over the last decade of the 1800s. Soccer survived those years in America mostly with the support of the many waves of immigrants that came to the United States at the end of the nineteenth century. The newly arrived Europeans brought with them their love for the kicking-form of football, and they kept it alive in neighborhood clubs.

Soccer was not a part of the daily lives of all Americans, but in some immigrant communities it certainly was. It thrived in the working class neighborhoods of New York City, Philadelphia, and parts of New Jersey.

American Football

American football has its beginnings on college campuses in the Northeastern states. In 1820, Princeton played a game called "ballown" that resembled American football, and Harvard had a tradition called "Bloody Monday" that began in 1827. But these games could hardly be called American football; they were more

like a game of soccer with lots of rough play than the passing, tackling, and touchdown sport we know today.

In the 1860s, '70s, and '80s, a series of meetings were held between the leaders of "football" on college campuses in the Northeast. A man named Walter Camp eventually attended these meetings; Camp would become the "father" of modern American football.

Camp's biggest contribution was a "line of scrimmage," which anyone who

watches football today will recognize as the defining mark of football. The line of scrimmage breaks play up into a series of "downs" in which the two teams form opposing lines before the ball enters play. The line helped football become a game of strategy as much as it was a game of raw strength. It took some of the more primitive, violent nature out of it and gave it a whole new appeal.

Football, however, would need many more years before society as a whole accepted it. Many people find it hard to believe that football—which draws more television viewers to its game than any sport in America—was still a relatively unpopular sport by the year 1900!

Walter Camp attended Yale from 1876 through 1880, where he was an avid football player.

Walter Camp became known as the Father of American Football. He was the dominant voice on the various collegiate football rules committees that developed the American game from his time as a player at Yale until his death.

Hockey

The formal version of the game we know as hockey today was still taking shape in the 1800s. It wasn't until the late 1870s that official rules would travel down from Canada and enter into American hockey play. Until then, hockey remained an informal game—but its players took it very seriously.

Hockey has a history of being a rough sport. Much like the early days of American football, hockey began as a mob game often played by all the men of neighboring villages. In Scotland and Ireland, where it was played on the dirt as often as it was on the ice, it was common for over a hundred men to make up a single team!

In its most basic form, hockey dates back thousands of years. At its core, hockey included many ball-and-stick games in which players with sticks push an object from one end of a surface to the other. Goal sizes varied, as did the team sizes and the type of object being

The Montreal Ice Hockey Club in 1888.

By the end of the nineteenth century, women had begun playing the game as well.

pushed. By the 1800s, Americans took the concept from Europe and adapted it to frozen ponds and lakes.

Ice skates of the 1800s were crude in comparison to today's version. As early as the 1300s, the Dutch had attached wooden platforms to iron runners, and by the 1800s, skates were being fitted with steel blades for faster movement. In 1859, a Canadian named James Whelpley developed a more comfortable skate that could be worn longer. Those who could afford skates bought them, but it was more common for hockey players to make their own—or simply play without them.

Hockey sticks were also still in development. Many players used straight sticks that fanned out toward one end. Legend says that one player broke his stick near the end, and then continued to play with the "L" shaped stick, only to find that it increased the accuracy and speed of his shots. However, the change actually came about, the "L"-shaped stick had become standard by the end of the 1800s.

A variation of hockey called "ice polo" became popular in the New England states. Ice polo has no off-side rule, meaning passes and shots on goal can come from all over the playing surface at any time. The puck is replaced with a rubber-covered ball, and usually the sticks are heavier. There are five players: a goal keeper, a half-hack, a center, and two rushers. The rushers must be quick and good at passing and scoring. The center

In the cold coastal regions of New England and Canada, communities could simply clear snow off the ice in the harbor for an instant playing field.

supports the rushers and controls the middle ground, and the half-hack is the last defender, along with the goalie.

Pond hockey could be played informally by kids getting together for a good time on a winter day.

Ice polo made it easier to play pick-up games of hockey in the cold weather of the Northern states, where ice was plentiful. So did pond hockey, which required no referees and could be fitted to any frozen surface. Professional hockey leagues

An amateur hockey league was established in 1896 in New York City. The team pictured here, the Crescent Hockey Team, were the champions of this league in 1911.

wouldn't exist until the early 1900s, and until then, hockey consisted of pick-up games and amateur rivalries between towns and neighborhoods. Today, the National Hockey League (NHL) is one of the major professional sports leagues in North America.

INCREDIBLE INDIVIDUAL
James Naismith, Inventor of Basketball

James Naismith was born in Ontario, Canada, in 1861. Orphaned at an early age, James was raised by his aunt and uncle, who recognized early on that the young boy had natural talent as an athlete. James excelled at wrestling, soccer, gymnastics, and football. One of his favorite childhood pastimes was a game called "duck on a rock" in which players try to knock over a large rock by throwing smaller rocks. James mastered the game by using a soft, arced shot instead of a fast, straight shot—a technique that would prove to be important to the creation of basketball.

His love of sports led James to earn a physical education degree from McGill University in Montreal. He went on from there and got a job at a YMCA in Springfield, Massachusetts. There, in the bitter New England winter, he was forced to create a new game to keep his bored students occupied indoors. James's boss told him to make up a game that was fair for all players and not too rough.

James went to work. His first concern was the ball. By thinking about the major sports of the time—rugby, lacrosse, soccer, football, hockey, baseball—he decided that a big ball was safest. He chose a soccer ball. Safety being his biggest concern, he also decided the game should be based on passing. That way no one would be injured by tackles or hits. Finally, he placed the goal high enough that no one could guard it. Players would need to use the soft, lobbing shot of James's childhood if they wanted to score goals.

In the first basketball games, peach baskets were used instead of baskets.

On the day that the first game of basketball was played, James posted his "13 Rules" on a bulletin board in the gymnasium. He attached two peach baskets about 10 feet from the floor on opposite sides of the court. At first, the students were confused. They didn't know quite how to pass, and many ignored the no-contact rules and tackled whoever held the ball. But the game slowly gained momentum. Within a few months, it was so popular that YMCAs around the country began adopting it and playing it competitively. By the turn of the century, Naismith would become the first college basketball coach at the University of Kansas. Although many of the rules would change over time, the basics of the sport were in place. Basketball had been born.

Golf

Credit for the invention of golf belongs to the Scottish, who have played the sport for over five hundred years. Some believe golf began with shepherds knocking stones into holes with their wooden crooks. Over time, as their skills increased, players increased the difficulty of the game by putting more distance between themselves and the hole.

As the rules become more advanced, so did the equipment, which made the game even more popular. King James I of England (1566-1625) was a golfer, and he commanded that golf balls be made for the royal court. At that time, and for the following centuries, golf balls had to be slowly and carefully made from feathers

stuffed into leather pouches. By the 1800s, however, rubber from India was introduced. Golfers were skeptical at first, and for good reason—the smooth balls tended to swerve around in the air. But experienced players soon realized that scratches and nicks put on the ball over time gave it more accuracy. The technique worked so well that it soon became common practice to score new balls with marks. By the end of the 1800s, the feather ball had been almost entirely replaced.

In 1888, a Scotsman named John Reid built the first three-hole course near his home

Harry Vardon was the first professional golfer to play in short pants called knickerbockers (the "proper" golfer dressed in an uncomfortable shirt and tie with a buttoned jacket). He became one of the first golf superstars, and in 1896, he won the first of his record six Open Championships (a record that still stands today).

in Yonkers, New York. Over the next decade, a handful of other courses were built outside Chicago and in the Southern states. Five courses came together in 1894 to form the group that would become the United States Golf Association (USGA), but golf wouldn't be played professionally until the next century.

As is still largely the case today, golf was an expensive sport, which limited its access to the lower classes. At first, this was based on the nature of the game itself, which required a lot of land to build courses. The "country-club" system was quickly put into place, requiring anyone interested in golfing to become a member of the course and pay a yearly fee.

As golf's popularity increased in the next century, more Americans gained access to the sport. But in the 1800s, it was relatively off-limits for all but the rich.

Union soldiers even played baseball when they were prisoners of war, as pictured here in the Salisbury, North Carolina, Confederate prison.

Baseball has a unique place in American history. From early on, something was different about the way Americans viewed this game. It was a team sport, but it put individuals in the spotlight: pitcher against batter, outfielder against a high fly ball. When Civil War soldiers played it in their camps, it reminded them of home and more peaceful times. Poor kids roaming city streets played it between buildings and in empty lots. Something about baseball was a perfect fit for the new nation. It became—and it remains—America's "Favorite Pastime."

Origins

Some argue that baseball came straight out of the English game of "rounders." Others say that baseball is uniquely, entirely American, and came from the games that American children played. As far as we know today, both sides are right. Somehow, in the late 1700s and early 1800s, the game of baseball emerged. It wasn't quite "rounders," and it wasn't quite a child's bat-and-ball game, either.

In the early years of the nineteenth century, baseball became the sport of choice for boys and girls both on farms and in the cities. For older men too, baseball was a favorite game. During the Civil War, Northern soldiers couldn't stop playing the game, even in a time of war, and it spread from them to the Southerners they encountered on and off the battlefield! Although many others games existed, baseball was the first sport unique to America to be played across the nation.

By the middle of the 1800s, baseball was a favorite sport for both adults and children in communities across America.

The first "official" game of baseball was played between the New York Knickerbockers and the New York Nine. The game was "official" because it was the first game it was played by agreed-upon rules. Alexander Cartwright, the founder of the Knickerbocker team, was the first man to write down a set of rules for how baseball should be played.

Cartwright wasn't the only one writing down rules. Men in other cities, like Philadelphia and Boston, were observing how baseball was played in their hometowns and writing down different sets of rules. The basic game stayed the same, but every hometown had its heroes and its own way of playing. There was "townball" in Philadelphia, "the Massachusetts game" in Boston, and "New York Style" in New York City.

The Equipment

When imagining those early days of baseball, you need to remember that modern equipment didn't exist. The beautifully shaped metallic and wooden bats we use today were nowhere to be found in 1846, when that first official game was played. But simplicity was part of the beauty. All you needed was a group of people, a ball, a bat, and an open space.

Simple things we take for granted—like baseball gloves—didn't become popular until the late 1800s. Some players began using unpadded gloves early on, especially the catcher and the first basemen, who received the most throws. But the average pitcher, outfielder, and infielder were likely to catch balls with their bare hands. Eventually, the idea caught on that padded gloves made the game more exciting. They allowed for harder throws and more spectacular catches.

Alexander Cartwright, the "Father of Baseball," who organized the first baseball club in 1845.

GLASSCOCK S.S.
INDIANAPOLIS

At first, people played baseball without a glove, as shown in this early baseball card

These early baseball players used bats and balls that looked a little different from the way they do today.

The ball itself evolved too. If you look at a baseball today, the first thing you notice are the red stitches around the white leather that make two circle patterns. This design has stayed the same for a surprisingly long time; the "figure-eight" stitch pattern was invented in 1872! The materials, however, have come a long way since those early days. In the 1840s, baseballs were basically a heavy core wrapped in padding and then sealed in a leather pouch. They were light, and hitting them long distances was not easy. Over time, the core became heavier, however, the padding firmer, and the leather pouch more reliable.

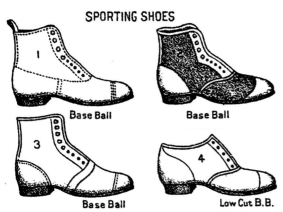

SPORTING SHOES

Base Ball

Base Ball

Base Ball

Low Cut B.B.

Nineteenth-century baseball shoes.

The baseball bat has its own story. In the early days bats were made from any wood available. They came in all shapes and sizes. The earliest meetings to decide baseball rules determined bats should be no longer than 42 inches—

and for a while, bats were made with one side flattened! A rule was quickly made to outlaw such bats, though, since they were unfair and allowed hitters too much of an advantage.

Bats were easy to make. Anyone could cut a large branch and carve it into a trusty bat (just another reason baseball was so popular among ordinary, working-class people). You didn't need to cash a paycheck to have your own bat. Of course, some bats were better than others. One company that was successful at selling baseball equipment was Spalding. They patented their "wagon tongue bat" after it became wildly popular. The company claimed their bats were made from actual wagon tongues (the wooden projections at the front of a wagon, where it is connected to the animal pulling it), adding yet more ties between American culture and the game of baseball.

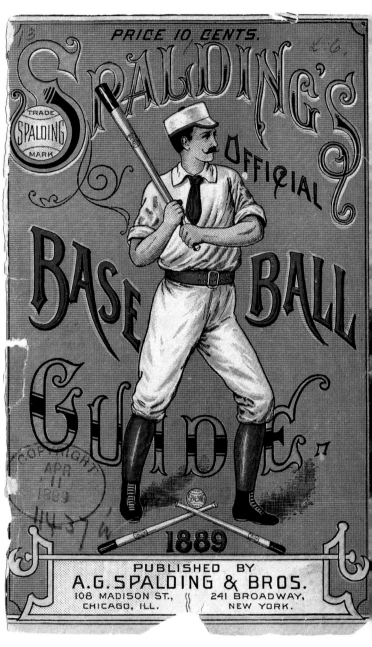

Spalding was the big name in baseball, right from the beginning. In 1889, they published the "official guide to baseball." Note that the book cost 10 cents!

L. F. Sockalexis.
H. C. C.
1900.

your friend.

INCREDIBLE INDIVIDUAL
Louis Sockalexis

Louis Sockalexis was born on the Penobscot Indian Reservation outside Old Town, Maine, in the year 1871. Louis's story belongs with a handful of athletes throughout history who bravely crossed racial lines for the first time.

From an early age, Louis showed promise as an athlete. He could run, catch, hit, and—so the legends say— throw the ball farther than anyone had ever seen a man throw. One story said that he once threw a ball over 600 feet across the Penobscot River. Whether or not that's accurate, one thing is true for certain: two Harvard professors measured one of his college throws at 414 feet in the air alone, meaning it traveled 414 feet before it hit the ground.

It wasn't long before major leagues came knocking on his door. In 1897 he signed a contract to play for the Cleveland Spiders in the National League.

Hardship came early on for Louis, however. Sadly, team owners were more impressed with Louis's ability to sell tickets than his talents on the field. They took every opportunity to play up Louis's Native roots. They described him as possessing "magic" powers, and encouraged fans to view him in a less than human light. Some stories describe fans making mock war cries, wearing feathers in their hair, and generally enjoying a joke at Louis's expense.

He continued to play well despite the distractions, but at the early age of twenty-five, tragedy struck him in the form of a broken ankle. Louis never quite recovered, and at twenty-seven, he retired. Louis never entirely gave up baseball, though. For the rest of his life, he continued to teach Native American boys the sport back on the Penobscot reservation of his childhood. Along with Jackie Robinson, who would become the first black player go professional almost fifty years later, Louis Sockalexis is remembered as a pioneer in the sport of baseball.

Professionalizing the Sport

Baseball owes much of its success to its early professionalism. "Professionalism" basically means paying players to play a sport, and baseball did that earlier than almost any other sport (or, at least, on a larger scale). As early as 1857, the National Association of Baseball Players formed, setting the stage for many leagues and games to come.

The advantage of professionally organizing the sport was simple: you could sell tickets! As teams became more organized, they became more competitive. They played hard, and they played to win. Not surprisingly, the games were fun to watch. Americans liked to watch heroes from their hometown (or even their neighborhood) play against the men from another city or town.

These games were exciting, and they offered a much needed distraction in the increasingly industrialized nation. Baseball was very popular among the working classes, especially among New York City's many immigrants.

As tickets started selling, the businessmen came into the picture. Probably a dozen or so different major leagues came and went in the years after the Civil War and before the creation of the National and American leagues in 1900 and 1901. Money brought corruption, of course. People had to be wary of "fixed matches," games in which one team deliberately lost to the other to satisfy gamblers.

Scandal almost swallowed up the sport, but it survived somehow. Soon nearly every city had its own baseball club. The Boston Red Stockings, the Chicago White Stockings, the St. Louis Brown Stockings, the Cincinnati Red Stockings (stockings were a big part of the baseball uniform!), New York Mutuals, Philadelphia Athletics, Louisville Grays, Boston Red Caps, and the Cleveland Forest Cities were just a few of the professional teams established before 1900. Every city wanted a team, and some cities had as many as three teams. It was official: baseball was here to stay.

Members of an early baseball team.

Rooting for the Home Team

The nineteenth century was an era without radio, television, or the Internet. Children who grew up playing baseball in the sandlots and open fields around their homes didn't go home to TV dinners to watch the New York Yankees on plasma screens. They had to find heroes closer to home.

Even though baseball was becoming a professional sport, kids still played the game whenever they had the chance.

Maybe that's why nineteenth-century baseball has such a unique place in American history. The baseball games of the 1800s were the first time that teams representing entire city populations played one another while spectators cheered them on. Never before in American history had the nation been interconnected enough for such a thing to occur. Now, suddenly, with railroad networks expanding and technology accelerating, people could play sports at the national level. Bragging rights were no longer just for the local bar; they were for the national pennant (the award given each year to the national champions in baseball).

People loved baseball enough to experiment with a new technology, electricity, just to be able to play it at night. Imagine: in the 1890s a few electrical companies attempted to provide electrical lights for the first night games! People went crazy with excitement. This was a whole new era for an America sport.

Other sports found their place in America in the 1800s—but baseball was America's sweetheart, it's very own game. As America grew, so did baseball. When Americans rooted for their home team, they knew they were also cheering for themselves . . . for America.

Think About It

Many of today's most popular amateur and professional sports have their roots in the 1800s. Baseball emerged as "America's Pastime" during this period.

- What is it about the game of baseball that made it so popular with Americans?

- Can you think of any specific things about the game—the pace at which it is played, the rules, the atmosphere of the ballpark, the makeup of the teams—that reflects the values of America in the 1800s?

In the twenty-first century, the number of fans and the amount of money generated by professional football has grown to be larger than baseball.

- What are some of the changes in American society that might have caused football to become more popular than baseball?

- What do you think might be the future of professional sports in America?

Words Used in This Book

bookmakers: People who take bets on sporting events, set the odds, and arrange payment for the winners.

carrier pigeons: Specially trained birds that carry messages from one place to another; before the invention of the telegraph it was one of the fastest methods of communication.

dueling: A method once used to settle a dispute between two people, in which they fought, usually with pistols or swords, until one of them was severely wounded or killed.

gruesome: Inspiring horror and disgust.

interconnected: Successfully united and working together.

lobbing: Hitting or throwing a ball in a high arc, a useful technique in many sports.

manifestation: The physical, visible expression of an idea.

scandals: Events that cause those involved public embarrassment and bad publicity.

superfluous: More of something than is necessary.

technology: The techniques and tools used in manufacturing, communication, transportation, and other human activities.

upstanding: Of excellent and respectable reputation.

vindicate: To prove the innocence of a person accused.

Find Out More

In Books

Crego, Robert. *Sports and Games of the 18th and 19th Century.* Westport, Conn.: Greenwood Press, 2003.

Peterson, Robert. *Pigskin: The Early Years of Pro Football.* Oxford, U.K.: Oxford University Press, 2007.

Sullivan, Dean. *Early Innings: A Documentary History of Baseball, 1825-1908.* Lincoln, Neb.: University of Nebraska Press, 1997.

On the Internet

American Soccer History
homepages.sover.net/~spectrum/overview.html

History of Basketball
library.thinkquest.org/10615/no-frames/basketball/history.html

John L. Sullivan, Champion Boxer
cyberboxingzone.com/boxing/sully.htm

Nineteenth Century Baseball
www.19cbaseball.com/

Who Invented Football
www.electro-mech.com/team-sports/football/who-invented-american-football

Index

Picture Credits

About the Author and the Consultant

Zachary Chastain is an independent writer and actor living in Binghamton, New York. He is the author of various educational books for both younger and older audiences.

John Gillis is a Rutgers University Professor of History Emeritus. A graduate of Amherst College and Stanford University, he has taught at Stanford, Princeton, University of California at Berkeley, as well as Rutgers. Gillis is well known for his work in social history, including pioneering studies of age relations, marriage, and family. The author or editor of ten books, he has also been a fellow at both St. Antony's College, Oxford, and Clare Hall, Cambridge.